Houses
and homes

Illustrations by Margaret Power

The blanket house

We have made

a house with chairs,

and we can sit inside.

The blanket goes

all around.

And makes a place to hide.

Jenny Giles

Willow tree house

I have a house,

My own little house,

Under the willow tree.

It's shady inside,

A good place to hide...

It's where I like to be.

Beverley Randell

4

Our apartment

We look out the window,
and we see the town.
The cars in the street,
are a long way down.

Beverley Randell

My little tent

My tent is so little,

With just room for one.

It keeps out the rain,

And it keeps out the sun.

It keeps out the wind,

And it keeps out the snow.

My tent is the best

Little house that I know.

Beverley Randell

Homes for tiny things

A tree has lots of little homes,

Homes for tiny things.

Tiny things with tiny legs,

And tiny things with wings.

Tiny things that hide away,

And tiny things that crawl.

A tree has lots of little homes,

A tree has homes for all.

Beverley Randell

The building song

Put up the walls,

Put down the floors,

Put in the windows,

And put in the doors.

Put on the roof,

Put in the stairs,

Take in the beds,

And the tables and chairs.

Beverley Randell

Baskets are for cats

Baskets are for cats,

Pillows are for dogs,

Burrows are for rabbits,

And puddles are for frogs.

A web is for a spider,

A hole is for a mouse,

A nest is for a bird,

But I live in a...

house.

Beverley Randell

Our house

Our house is a very good house.

It's a very good place to be.

And I have a room

where I sleep and play.

It's a room that's just for me.

Jenny Giles